Forest Animals

THIS BOOK BELONGS TO:
_ _ _ _ _ _ _ _ _

African animal: Giraffe

Coloring pages

African animal: Giraffe

African animal: Antelope

Coloring pages

African animal: Antelope

African animal: Elephant

Coloring pages

African animal: Elephant

African animal: Zebra

Coloring pages

African animal: Zebra

African animal: Vulture

Coloring pages

African animal: Vulture

African animal: Hippo

Coloring pages

African animal: Hippo

African animal: Leopard

Coloring pages

African animal: Leopard

African animal: Gorilla

Coloring pages

African animal: Gorilla

African animal: Lion

Coloring pages

African animal: Lion

Wild animal: Tiger

Coloring pages

Wild animal: Tiger

Wild animal: Wolf

Coloring pages:

Wild animal: Wolf

Wild animal: Bear

Coloring pages:

Wild animal: Bear

Wild animal: Cougar

Coloring pages:

Wild animal: Cougar

Wild animal: Deer

Coloring pages:

Wild animal: Deer

Wild animal: Fox

Coloring pages:

Wild animal: Fox

Wild animal: Hare

Coloring pages:

Wild animal: Hare

Wild animal: Argali

Coloring pages:

Wild animal: Argali

Wild animal: Llama

Coloring pages:

Wild animal: Llama

Wild animal: Lynx

Coloring pages:

Wild animal: Lynx

Wild animal: Moose

Coloring pages:

Wild animal: Moose

Thank you for choosing our book
We hope you enjoyed it !